SYNCHRONICITY "MY STORY"

JOHN A. HOUSE, CHFC

Balboa Press books may be ordered through booksellers or by contacting:

Balboa Press
A Division of Hay House
1663 Liberty Drive
Bloomington, IN 47403
www.balboapress.com
1 (877) 407-4847

Print information available on the last page.

ISBN: 978-1-9822-0334-4 (sc)
ISBN: 978-1-9822-0335-1 (hc)
ISBN: 978-1-9822-0348-1 (e)

Library of Congress Control Number: 2018905297

Balboa Press rev. date: 06/23/2018

CONTENTS

PREFACE

The purpose of "my story" is to offer tangible insights to a prospective client, their attorney or CPA on my character, values and personality traits. Notwithstanding the practice of medicine, I believe advising individuals, families and business owners on money matters is the next top lifetime responsibility! So, I ask, what is the most important personality trait of a financial adviser? The answer, with zero ambiguity, is personal integrity. Integrity is the foundation of a trusting relationship! Certainly competence and experience are essential components of a financial consulting practitioner, yet without honesty and the ability to focus on the best interests of another, one is at risk.

Since trust and personal integrity are difficult to access, we must rely on own ability to judge, as well as obtain the good opinion (experience) of others. When you are blessed with a viable friendship, the knowledge of one's past is usually an essential component of the relationship.

Therefore, my hope in sharing "My Story" is to compliment the intuitive with facts and circumstances. One of my foundation principles is the firm belief in synchronicity, "things in life happen for a reason." I feel that I am today living proof of God's will. I am still a student, who is passionately seeking more knowledge of mind, body and spirit. I approach each day with the following acknowledgments: "Have fun, be happy, stay healthy and do good!" I also try to always appreciate Dr. Wayne Dyer's thought provoking advice "If you change the way you look at things, the things you look at will change." I make the constant effort not to be judgmental and practice humility by remembering Walter Lippmann's quote: "First we look, then we name and only then do we see."

CHAPTER ONE

I am a survivor! I believe I still hold the record at the Onawa, Iowa Community Hospital as their longest surviving blue baby! At birth, I went four minutes and forty-seven seconds without breathing. My father was teasingly accused of chasing the nurse around the hospital for that magical shot that commenced my first breath.

As a young child, I was fortunate to be stationed in Utah with my mother and father. My dad had joined the Navy. Fortunately, my uniform did not qualify me for active duty!

I was blessed with two wonderful parents who were married for seventy years, only to be separated by my fathers demise at age 95. Mom is doing well and enjoys good health.

As a young boy I liked things on wheels as evidenced by the photo below!

I developed an entrepreneurial perspective through the building and sale of first stage Go-Carts. I initially financed this endeavor by using a push mower to mow yards. I discovered that if the blades were removed from the push reel mower I could install a pulley, which became the foundation of my Go-Cart business. My first engine was a one cycle Maytag washing machine motor, which was mounted above the reel mower apparatus. My clutch mechanism was variable, which allowed higher speeds. At the age of eleven, I was escorted to my home by a friendly policeman, who told my parents that I was speeding down 10th street! I eventually graduated into making custom go-carts and developed a profitable enterprise! I also became attracted to horses, which became a reality in later life. The horse picture below would ultimately lead to my ownership today of a majestic Friesian!

One of the most important attributes that I gleaned from my father was a strong work ethic!

My dad's dedication to his business, was multifaceted with a continuous expansion of product mix, that resulted in a community dominance. I began working for him at age twelve and found myself on nearly every assignment attempting to exceed his expectations. Recognition for my accomplishments was seldom represented, yet I continued to manifest a firm belief in doing the best I could. My dad acquired the first ice machines in our small Iowa town that produced 400 pounds of ice a day. I was responsible for creating an inventory of ten-pound bags for a market demand that exceeded production capacities. In recollection, I am certain that I approached scooping a million pounds of ice over the years.

At age thirteen I began boxing lessons offered by a former heavy weight champion who was recognized nationally for his career accomplishments. Physical conditioning superseded everything. Prior to my training with Ray, I held the record for one semester for being called to the principal's office seven times for fighting. Now, I had an avenue that captured my physical propensity and converted it into a viable channel. I worked hard and qualified for the Golden Gloves tournament only to be defeated in my championship match by a young man three years my senior, but holding the same weight class. It was a humbling experience that helped me matriculate into other athletic endeavors.

During the summer before my first year at the University of Iowa at age 18, I applied along with seventeen other young men for a construction job dedicated to a new building for the Monona County Rural Electric Association. I was among the two individuals selected and began with our first job of manually unloading 24,000 bricks from a train car to a truck. We would carry with two prongs fourteen bricks at a time until the truck was full. Then we had to unload the truck onto pallets at the job site! My arms grew longer and stronger!

Our foreman had assigned one of the carpenters the duty of building an outhouse on the construction site. On the weekend of completion, I decided that the little building needed some enhancements…..insights into my creative side! I began with the purchase of some brightly colored shingles, which I installed. Next a gallon of purple paint gave the outhouse a new identity. On the inside I installed cotton stuffed pink plastic fabric around the seats. As my next enhancement, I attached four playboy centerfolds to the inside walls. On the outside of the building I designed with yellow paint a half moon on the door. The final touch was the installation of a thirty-foot wrought iron pole with a Confederate flag. The reception by the construction crew on the following Monday was indeed hilarious. Our foreman mandated a picture of himself next to the outhouse. At later phases of our construction project, our foreman would take visitors on tours and always highlight the outhouse as a symbol of prestige!

Our biggest challenge after the concrete floors had been poured for the office area of the complex, was to recover the plywood support sections and two-by-four support arms. It was a hot summer and during the concrete curing process, extensive water was supplied, which eventually found its way to the crawl space under the floor. For two weeks, flat on our backs on pieces of styrofoam, the two of us (construction rookies) were assigned the job of removing the plywood and bringing it to one of the floors portals for final extraction. The removal process often resulted in the plywood falling on our bodies, frequently with protruding nails. We guesstimated the temperature under the concrete floor to be 105 degrees. We both lost ten to fifteen pounds during this phase of the project. There were many times when I considered going back to my dad's business, but tenacity prevailed.

Our final project was providing properly tamped "mud" to multiple brick layers. If the "mud" was not of the proper consistency at all times we would be chastised with a multitude of very descriptive adjectives!

My take-a-way was the transportation of my construction boots to the University of Iowa as motivation to study. Whenever, I procrastinated about my studies, I would carefully view my boots and vividly recall my construction job. To this day I firmly believe that my first-year grade point average of 3.7 was not attributed to intelligence; but rather to fear!

During my junior year of college, I sought employment with Bremers Clothing store in Iowa City. At the time, I had no idea that Bremers was the best men's store in Iowa, but I benefited from the two owners who were both past military officers. Discipline and orderliness were omnipotent requirements. Plus, I discovered some talent for fashion and quickly became the number one part time sales associate. The 1% commission on our individual sales handsomely rewarded my sales efforts.

Because of summer vacation, Iowa City turned into a morgue. Consequently, my sales career at Bremers was delayed until fall. At the age of 21, it was possible to acquire an insurance License in Iowa, so I answered a newspaper ad for a job with Globe Life & Accident Insurance Company. The goal after a one week intensive training program was to go door to door in towns throughout Iowa and sell residents Accident and Health Insurance. My father cautiously warned me that door to door sales was difficult and I should consider working for the family business. Notwithstanding my father's apprehension, I decided to join our unit of five sales men and begin my pursuit of commission. Globe Life did pay for our motel rooms. I found myself driving around town during my first two weeks of this business endeavor, reluctant to knock on anyone's door. Finally, I drove into the country and pulled into a farm yard owned and operated by Raymond Lang. As I began my unseasoned sales pitch, I could sense that Mr. Lang felt compassion for my efforts. He asked to see my "pitch book" and found an application and proceeded to complete the same, subject to my total bewilderment. I had made my first sale, which commenced the foundation of a life-long vocation!

From that moment, my fears dissipated. During the next week I convinced an older German couple to open their living room safe (with my back turned) to retrieve their Continual Casualty Accident and Health policy for me to review. The annual premium was around $200. Total benefits, based upon a catastrophe medical condition resulted in a complete payout of just $600.00. Their hospital ten dollar a day benefit was $300.00. Our Globe policy provided $30.00 a day for a full year with a similar premium. Once I could tangibly demonstrate the differences, they agreed to cancel their old contract and purchased mine. Now, not only had

I improved their coverage dramatically; but I had developed a deep passion and a sense of purpose to help other people with similar outdated policies. Over the next ten weeks I replaced 73 insurance contracts. My compensatory rewards were staggering! And, then I learned that I would receive renewals each time the insured paid another premium. I was literally in insurance heaven!

Upon my return to college, I truly felt wealthy! I think my financial independence made me a better salesman… I had more confidence. I went back to the University of Iowa and reduced my academic hours and began working more at Bremers. I also tried to recruit accident and health Insurance clients, but soon discovered "city folks" to be more resistant in allowing a stranger to penetrate their home environment! To this day, I think folks from small towns are friendlier!

One of my academic challenges, was meeting the requirement of a foreign language. I always assumed good English would be enough! I reluctantly chose Spanish. And, since I was working at Bremers nearly full time, I continued to procrastinate. Finally, after entering graduate school in the field of economics it became fundamentally clear to me that I must complete Spanish to obtain my Bachelor of Science degree in Sociology. After help from several tutors from the Spanish department, I was able to barely pass the first semester with a D. As I entered my final year at Iowa, I was only taking one undergraduate course...Spanish! I had passed the first test; but failed the midterm. The Spanish department candidly informed me that I must achieve a C on the final to pass. I was desperate! The only salvation was the limited scope of the final. There were a few short stories to interpret, a 110-page novel and five outlines of verbs and adjectives. So, I decided two weeks before the final to take a leave of absence from Bremers and study. Since I had no idea how to really learn a language, I chose to memorize everything. I slept an average of four hours a night for two weeks. Come the day of the test...I was ready! The final was in an auditorium, where we were nicely separated to avoid collusion. As the screen popped up with Spanish terms, we were instructed to interpret. The further into the test I proceeded, the more confident I felt! I was going to nail this exam. Fear, again had aided my learning experience!

Two weeks later the grades were posted and I had achieved an "A" on the final exam, which meant I could graduate and accomplish my first degree! I was surprised when I received a note from Dr. Gonzales, the head of the Spanish department, that he would like to see me. To my astonishment, I learned that I needed to support my A grade! After setting up a meeting, I went to the Spanish Department office and sat in front of Dr. Gonzales and the two of the graduate students, who I had previously hired as tutors. There was little happiness in this office!

I was told that based upon my previous grading experience in the language of Spanish that it would be very difficult for me to achieve a A grade on the final exam, and therefore they were interested in how I had accomplished such a substantial improvement! I seriously looked Dr. Gonzales straight in the eye and asked him to find the 110-page novel that was the part of the exam. Once he did, I respectfully suggested that at random he select any page in the book and read to me the first sentence. To his absolute bewilderment and the astonishment of my tutors, I quoted the remainder of the page in its entirety…and graduated!

CHAPTER TWO

Self-confidence is an interesting phenomenon. I had experienced mostly good relationships with university women. As the social chairman of my fraternity for five years, I was in an ideal position to meet and date a variety of women. Notwithstanding being rejected (dumped) by my pin mate as a junior, when she became Iowa's Homecoming Queen, I enjoyed positive experiences. Approaching my final year as a student and participating in many classmates' weddings, I concluded that I should find a wife before entering the non-academic world. I did! She was five years younger than me and her dentist father wanted her to finish college.

Bremers clothing and insurance commissions were not sufficient to support my new marriage, and other vocational opportunities in Iowa City were rather limited. Fortunately,

Montgomery Ward was opening a large store in a new Iowa City shopping center. I interviewed, and with my retail clothing background, was hired with a salary that would support my marriage. There was however a significant adjustment, due to a dramatic change in targeted customer. Bremers sought the elite, whereas Montgomery Ward dedicated their marketing to mainstream America.

After serving for two months as a management trainee, I was assigned to Montgomery Wards men's department. I had developed a good working relationship with our store manager. He respected my focus and strong work ethic, which was partially personified in my plus seventy hours of work every week.

With my recent status as a graduating student, I knew from my work at Bremers the protocol of graduation. For our male students, it was the purchase of a suit to accommodate employment interviews. Because the price of clothing at Bremers made it difficult for the average financially struggling senior to acquire a new suit, I felt that there was a market for lower priced clothing. As part of my new job I would attend in Kansas City the Montgomery Ward semi-annual buying event. Ironically, the hotel included a Playboy Club!

I was able to obtain a pass the night before our business meeting and found myself somewhat enthralled by the female ambiance! Soon I was at a pool table playing pool with an attractive Bunny. She convinced me to try their new drink called "Herbe". The drink came with a nifty (free) mug. I remember finding my room okay, but when I woke up the next morning my vision was really blurry. Had the "Herbe" drink caused blindness? Then I discovered that my contact lenses were still in my eyes. What a relief!

In retrospect, I was not at my optimal self for the buying experience, yet I did discover an attractive suit vendor, with a great price structure. I could buy a 100% wool gabardine, three piece vested suit at a price that could be successfully (profitably) promoted at $99. My department budget would accommodate fifty to sixty suits. My idea was to run a double truck (two full newspaper pages) ten weeks prior to graduation and sell several hundred suits, so I purchased twelve hundred. I was confident that my store manager would approve the order, once I explained to him my promotional plans. Fortunately for me, my manager was progressive and after a persuasive conversation, he agreed to approve my suit order. The promotion was extremely successful, and our men's department ranked number one in the country for three separate months. After only seven months I was promoted to Merchandise Manager, whereupon I managed eighteen departments or half of the whole store.

One of my Bremer friends felt empathy for me having moved from the sale of high quality clothing to lower end ready-to-wear and suggested that I contact the Dayton Department Store in Minneapolis and explore a marketing career with them. I was overwhelmed by my duties at Wards (the extremely long hours) and welcomed the opportunity to explore vocational endeavors with one of the top department stores in the country. My interview went very well, and Dayton's paid for my moving/relocation expenses. After three months as a management trainee, I was promoted to an assistant department manager. I was now deeply entrenched in the marketing of furnishings (dress shirts, neckwear and accessories). For whatever reason my predecessors had not liked to handle returned items (charge backs to the manufacturing venders) and I discovered in our Section of the 10th Floor Storage Facility, hundreds of defective dress shirts and ties that were included in our inventory, which negatively impacted my buyers Open to Buy. I decided to tackle the charge back opportunity and spent nearly eight weeks at nights separating, pricing and packing up distressed merchandise. The result was an extra $23,000 in "new" Open to Buy. Ultimately, I was rewarded with one of the highest (point scores) annual reviews in Dayton's history for an assistant buyer. I was next promoted to a sales manager's role at the downtown St. Paul, Minnesota store. I oversaw 73 employees and was given the assignment of improving sales in the entire men's division in a store that ranked at the bottom of the six-store operation. Understandably, our buyers treated St. Paul as a step child and were reluctant to provide inventory when compared to the high profile shopping center stores. Consequently, I needed to develop a strategy to obtain a broader and more in-depth inventory position. My roundtrip drive (with traffic) each day was over sixty miles. I also needed to get back to the Minneapolis store, which could only happen through a promotion. There were 68 trainees in our training class the year that I started my career at Dayton's and as it turned out only four of us became buyers!

Since my tenure in St. Paul was just preparatory to the holiday season, I decided to create my own type of inventory or better said----product offering. Late at night I would arrive at our Minneapolis store and carefully select merchandise, which I subsequently loaded into hampers with the proper documentation. The hampers would arrive in St. Paul the next day. My selections were such that the downtown sales managers did not recognize or sense the depletion in their respective inventories--- a real benefit to my endeavors. Not surprisingly, St. Paul's Dayton store was hungry for a broader and more in-depth selection of inventory. At the end of the Christmas season we had become the number one store in our six-store group with the highest percentage of sales increase over the previous year. In early January I was apprised of a lateral promotion as assistant buyer in Dayton's Lady's handbag department. The buyer was a twenty-three-year veteran and was recognized across the department store country as one of the top performers. I enthusiastically accepting every assignment with a smile and dedication for completion. I would be seen through the three floors of the Dayton's Minneapolis store diligently carrying twenty to twenty five handbags on each arm as I was constantly instructed to change the inventory displays. My buyer believed that relocating hand bags every day would improve her sales.

After four months I was beginning to impress my buyer with a good work ethic, astute listening skills (I took her directions well) and tenacity. However, after two years of essentially being an apprentice, I was still not wearing the buyers badge. My frustration culminated one Monday afternoon when I ran into Dayton's first non-family member, store president. He held a master's degree from Harvard's business college and was extremely well respected by all the buyers and other executive leaders. When he greeted me warmly and asked with authenticity how I was doing, I responded with…not very well! Additionally, I indicated that I planned to resign from Dayton's, since I did not believe that management recognized my talents to be a buyer. After a thoughtful moment, he asked if I would wait until Friday to officially resign. I responded with a sure…what would four more days mean? I had no other vocational plans and the thought (a reality check) of being unemployed was a little scary!

Interestingly, on Friday afternoon I got a call from the director of recruitment, the man who originally hired me, to report to his office. To make a long story short, on that day I was made buyer of the Young Men's Varsity Shop.

The previous buyer was promoted to a merchandise manager over half of the men's division. It was difficult to hide my excitement and sense of relief from achieving my goal of becoming a Dayton buyer!

The next thing I remember was a request from Dayton's travel center to schedule my first buying trip to New York. Wow! I had never been to Manhattan; and to think I was to be there one week of almost every month as a buyer. I commenced an immediate effort to understand the "numbers" of my Varsity Shop. At that historic stage, retail technology was just beginning to materialize. I knew that I was responsible for understanding the key statistical ratios of my department. I vividly recalled the experience of a buyer who was asked the question at a management meeting: "where would you rank this item in our Trend Schedule?"

Dayton's had developed a methodology of tracking, evaluating and then taking specific inventory action. Each item of merchandise would be identified by color, fabric, and style. As a buyer you were obligated to have approximately 5% of your entire inventory in the "testing mode", 15% in an "incoming stage" and 60% in between "pre-peak" and "post peak", with the balance in "outgoing"...whereupon mark downs would be instigated.

A garment style could be in the "pre-peak" stage and the color could be "outgoing". Management wanted to know from all Buyer/Department Managers where their respective key items ranked on this hypothetical Trend Schedule or chart. The buyer I referenced above, a Rhodes Scholar from England answered the question at a store management meeting with: "Oh, it is way up there on the trend chart." Everyone gasped internally. Two weeks later that buyer was history!

Accordingly, I recognized that my responsibility was not only to buy the right merchandise in the right quantities for each of our six stores, but know how it was always performing! Rate of sale data was omnipotent!

Because of my limited cultural background growing up in a small Iowa town I decided to attend plays in New York during my evenings there. Vendors would provide dinners, drinks, and theater tickets, which remained in bounds for the accepted gift protocol. Of course, everyone wanted Dayton's business and would do their very best to convince Dayton buyers of the value of their respective products. I was enthralled with Broadway and absolutely wowed by my theatrical experience.

It was interesting and important that we belonged to the Assorted Merchandising Association (AMA), which was supported by the top twenty-five department stores in America. As a buying group, the AMA would generate private label merchandise opportunities for its member buyers, which were generally of high quality and favorably priced, often from overseas market places.

On the scary side of the coin, each buyer's department was compared to every other department of like kind among all the other AMA associated department stores. I knew that the challenge of competing with Richs in Atlanta, Abraham and Strauss in New York and Neiman Marcus in Dallas would be difficult, since Minneapolis was not considered a major metropolitan market place. My endeavors would be measured with public number comparisons; not just good performance in Minnesota. Our constant challenge as buyers was being overbought on paper and with real inventory. There was a constant conflict of maximizing sales growth and profitably with the most clothing inventory one could acquire. The greater the amount of inventory, usually the better our performance.

In my first year, I was competitive on a national basis and my Varsity Shop was profitable. I had become reasonably proficient in my new role and was surprised when our store president scheduled a meeting and asked me if I could help him and Dayton's with a community oriented project. Of course, I responded positively and asked him what they wanted me to do? He explained that Dayton's had aligned itself with the Urban Coalition League and as a result certain buyers were being asked to help independent Black American retailer store owners two days a week.

My first reaction was selfish! How would I be able to achieve my Varsity Shop bonus by working in the store only four days of the week? I usually worked on Saturdays and Sunday was my day for rest and relaxation. Our president recognized my slight dismay and said the following: "John, let me share my vocational philosophy with you and how you will do better by spending two less days a week on the job. First, focus on your strengths and maximize them. Next, focus on your departments weaknesses and improve or resolve them. Then leave everything in the middle essentially alone. Next, learn to better delegate and empower your staff with responsibility. The results will become self-evident." "And, recognize, John that you were carefully chosen for this role." I immediately felt a combined sense of relief and confidence. Carl Erickson, our store president, was an exceptional individual and an awesome leader. His confidence in me was a little overwhelming!

My introduction to Joe, my first store owner to help on Hennepin Avenue was interesting. As I walked into his store I encountered a jam session in the shoe department. Joe was a professional saxophone player and he was good. As the group disassembled I introduced myself to Joe and he invited me to his office. Feeling a little awkward, I posed a number of questions, then shared some background information. I explained my appointment and how the Urban Coalition League was postured to help. Joe had received a $150,000 grant to open his men's store, yet had no retail experience, other than being a sophisticated, well-dressed customer to several high-end men's stores. Without retail training and an open mind, we both readily concluded that his business could be improved. Something as fundamental as shoe sizing, was our first project. Joe had purchased from a famous Italian shoe maker several styles that were very saleable, yet he had acquired an equal quantity in each size. He had as many 8 ½

C's as he had 10 ½ C's. We were able to convince the vendor to exchange each style for a more well-balanced and sized inventory. And, the results were formable!

We worked diligently on some promotional plans and applied for additional funding. Together we were able to turn Joe's business into a profitable retail enterprise! I actually felt more pride and satisfaction in helping Joe, than in the profitable operation of my Varsity Shop! Thank you, Carl!

Back at Dayton's I had become rather proficient at delegating, and to my surprise with really good results. As long as I carefully explained to my staff each project with predetermined accountability, and posed good questions it appeared to me that everyone's commitment to success was growing. The take-a-way principle became the foundation for future business success--- treat your team members with respect, request their qualified feedback and opinions, identify methods of accountability, jointly prioritize time frames for projects and proficiently recognize (reward) accomplishments-----celebrate the results of planned outcomes.

It also became apparent to me, that the problems and challenges I face should be perceived as opportunities with the hope of making me stronger and smarter verses being bogged down by negativity. I began to recognize and understand that our attitude is a choice and we can actually choose our reaction to each life situation.

I had grown to believe that anything of genuine quality in life can be accomplished through a step by step process, whereupon good, well thought through choices on a daily basis will produce desired outcomes.

The above referenced thoughts remind me of a famous quote: *"If you are stressed by anything external, the pain or concern is not due to the thing or situation itself, but to your estimate of it; and this you have the power to revoke at any moment!"*

Going back to the successful operation of the Varsity Shop, and as a natural born risk taker, I found myself in an awkward corporate situation, based upon an aggressive New York buying decision. Or better said, in trouble. The biggest sale of the year was Dayton's Jubilee promotion. It was held in October every year and usually produced profits equivalent to the pre-Christmas weeks in December.

While on a buying trip in New York I was invited to a mill in New Haven, Connecticut, where both Robert Bruce and Jantzen sportswear were manufactured. At that particular time in retail, Robert Bruce, who was promoted by Arnold Palmer and Jantzen were considered top national name brands. During my tour of the mill one of the owners asked if I would be interested in reviewing a promotional merchandise offering from these two famous vendors. Of course, I responded and was lead to a lavish show room. Both manufactures, during the production phase of making velour shirts and matching slacks had experienced problems with the fabric, resulting in barely discernable flaws. As a result, massive quantities were being offered as "seconds" at exceptional price points. I envisioned a huge promotion for the Varsity Shop Jubilee Sale!

The offering was an all or nothing and if I was interested the orders had to be initiated now. Based upon the price, the brand and the markup potential, I wrote an order that was sufficient to fill up two semi-trucks-----1900 dozen for one shipment and 1000 dozen for a second or backup shipment. Dayton's merchandising procedure was to construct your hypothetical orders in New York and then return and review them with your Divisional Merchandise Manager for approval before formal placement. I was confident that I could convince my Divisional Merchandise Manager (DMM) to authorize these orders, based upon the marketing merits and pricing, even though I was over bought on paper. Unfortunately, I was wrong… the orders would not be authorized. I decided not to disclose that the vendor (the Mill) had signed purchase orders, because I hoped to get them signed prior to the Jubilee sale, assuming good sales would resolve my over-bought position---wishful thinking. I fully recognized that buyers could be fired for issuing unauthorized purchase orders, a true dilemma, just waiting to happen.

The week before the Jubilee sale the first semi-truck pulled into the sub-basement of Dayton's downtown receiving docks and was checked in with a traffic control number (TCN). Understandably, with no matching purchase order a "deviation" occurred! Because of the large quantity of merchandise, the deviation went directly to Ken Macke's office, our Retail Store Senior Vice President. (Ken later became the chairman of Dayton Hudson/Target stores)

Ken was from Carol, Iowa and had played college football. I remember that his eyes were vibrant and penetrating. I explained my actions and respectfully suggested that he should authorize the TCN deviation and accept the merchandise, since Dayton's legally owned it. When I left his office, I was still employed for the moment? And, fortunately he had authorized acceptance of my order, based upon my promise to have amazing results!

After the first two days of the Jubilee sale my Jantzen and Roberts Bruce velour shirts and slacks had experienced a near 80% sale through with a triple digit price mark up. Ken called me into his office and in a humble manner asked if I could get any more from the Mill. I proudly handed him the second TCN deviation that was in the sub-basement. I will never forget his look and what he called me! And, as evidence by this writing---I was not fired!

One of our many challenges as a buyer was the control of both external and internal theft. Our young men's varsity shop was a target market for theft which resulted in inventory shrinkage, which adversely impacts profitability. My predecessor had warned me of the theft factor and provided vivid examples. The Southdale Dayton's store in the heart of Edina Minnesota was our most prolific branch store. I learned that the year before an entire portable stereo system had been stolen. Of my $4,500,000 in sales volume, inventory shrinkage was running at nearly 4.0% of sales. One of our top selling categories were young men's leather jackets. It was easy to discern from the comparison of registered sales to inventory that more than 10% of the jackets were being stolen; not sold!

I may not have been first in the nation, but I was certainly early in the process when I asked our carpenter department on the tenth floor of our Downtown Minneapolis store to be creative. I directed them to weld hooks on the T-Stand display that would allow wires through leather coat sleeves with padlocks for security. I can vividly recall visiting our St. Paul store who had been allocated one of my new secure T-Stands and 10 Leather Bomber styled jackets. When I could not find recorded cash register sales nor the jackets, I discovered that the entire T-stand had disappeared (been stolen) with all ten the leather jackets safely padlocked.

Our Downtown store employed twenty five full time protection personnel to discourage theft. Being perplexed and concerned by my anticipated inventory shortage I began the process of intercepting "private label" denim jeans and taking an extra $2.00 to $3.00 in mark ups, which I recorded in my markup/mark down register. One hundred dozen jeans gave me a $2400 to $3600 theft cushion, which would help me improve my department's gross margin. I carefully executed this practice for the entire fall season, resulting in a substantial cumulative mark up. Unfortunately, in discussions with my Divisional Merchandise Manager, I was informed that it was mandatory for me to report or turn in my markup for the year. I reluctantly complied and in early January was asked to meet privately with our new store president…an unusual request for a buyer. I discovered at the meeting, which also included out store Vice President, that my Varsity Shop had recorded the highest gross margin in the country, when compared with the other twenty five AMA department store organizations who, operated young men's varsity shops. As noted previously, through the AMA everyone's numbers were reported and open to management scrutiny. And, they wanted to know how I did it! My response was succinct and truthful. I was forced to mitigate my strategy to reduce my inventory shrinkage numbers and report all booked mark ups. They readily understood and made a store wide directive to all buyers that "Key Stone" markup (traditionally 50%) was not an absolute and that discretion (increase your markup percentage) should be employed on privately labeled merchandise.

Needless to say, I achieved an amazing year-end review and received a significant bonus.

CHAPTER THREE

Simultaneous to my fourth Annual Dayton's review, I was introduced to Galen Skramstad, by one of my favorite wholesale vendors. Galen had failed to qualify on the professional golf circuit and decided, with the help of his wealthy spouse, to enter the retail clothing business. Other than growing up as a phenomenal athlete and a scratch golfer, he enjoyed no retail experience. His father, however was a successful men's store owner and with his partner, Bill Wilson had six stores. Interestingly, Galen exuded a Burt Reynold's styled personality, and a great sense of humor!

I would be his technician (merchandiser and buyer) and become his partner if he could convince me to leave Dayton's and join him. His master plan was dedicated to the opening of nine men's stores and six lady's stores in four states. I was truly enthralled by the opportunity to become a 30% shareholder, as a signing bonus for one large store with an option to purchase additional shares (capped at 49% ownership) and then help merchandise the other stores. At that time, Galen had limited background in the marketing of men's and ladies clothing. Importantly, he aspired towards high quality and appreciated the merchandising experience that I brought to the table.

Although, I thoroughly enjoyed my experience at Dayton's I was aware that our corporate environment could be completely changed through different management. I also liked the idea of moving into a smaller community...a town with five connected lakes.

My challenge would be the transitional timeframe. The lead time for the acquisition of men's suits was four to five months, plus the men's and ladies stores (9000 sq. ft. of space) had to be built out to our specifications. Then we had to design our fixtures. Fortunately, Galen had opened his first store the year before in Mankato, Minnesota and had developed a number of good vendor relationships. Because I was in New York for one week every month, I would combine my Varsity Shop buying responsibilities with the acquisition of merchandise for both of the new stores.

A friend in New York had introduced me to a popular bar/restaurant named Dimension. I subsequently, convinced Galen to let me name our ladies division "dimension". The men's store would be called Wilsons, based upon Galen's father's business relationship with a partner, Bill Wilson. After several months of preparation and merchandise buying, I was ready to resign my buyer's job at Dayton's. We had found a home, began some furnishing purchases and had signed a ten-year lease for our shopping center space. Unfortunately, I did not anticipate the difficulty I would encounter with the resignation process at Dayton's. After submitting my one-month departure date, I was called into our store president's office along with our vice president of marketing and told that I was slated to be the buyer of the men's furnishings division with double the sales volume of the Varsity shop! In addition, it would mean an immediate and significant increase in compensation. I simply explained that I had made an absolute personal commitment to my partner and I did not wish to deviate from the integrity of that relationship. They wished me well in my new endeavor!

We had planned for our stores to open in August and we were on target to accomplish the same. It was an exciting adventure--- especially as an owner. The community warmly greeted us. My wife at that time, Barbara, mother to our three-year-old daughter, Jacqueline, had theatrical talent and immediately became involved in community arts programs.

In my first year in business three community leaders convinced me to invest $2500 in Fairmont Growth Opportunities Inc. a 260-acre industrial park designed to attract industry to Fairmont. Since our funds were limited, they accommodated a five year payback with no interest. My marketing skills were paying off and both stores were doing well in spite of some good competition. I had hired a friend from Minneapolis, who worked for Dayton's display department to do our store windows every three weeks. The results of his work were outstanding. We had the best window displays within a fifty-mile radius.

Our retail business continued to survive, although we were not doing very well at retiring debt. At one point in my new retail career I considered the option of writing a book called Market Trip! We truly had lots of fun when all of our store managers attended buying trips. I will share one experience that was memorable. We were attending a market trip in Houston. I was single at that time and my partner Galen was separated from his wife, Suzan.

The Menswear Retailers of America market show was being held in the Houston Astro Dome and as usual the clothing vendors had set up display booths along with promotional activities that allowed us as buyers to participate and compete. For example, Fran Tarkington and YA Title, two former NFL quarterbacks were throwing a football through a moving tire on a rope at a pretty good distance and speed. They were really good. Galen had been an accomplished high school quarterback and was successful in winning a prize for his score. We were a very competitive group; especially Galen and me!

Our next contest was to ride a stationary bicycle for five minutes and see who could go the furthest…the prize was a small color TV. Galen and I decided to make it a life or death competition. I had been blessed with extremely strong thighs and I was sure I could win. Two thirds of the way through our race, I proudly proclaimed that I was going so fast, that I was creating smoke! Seriously, my tire was smoking! As it turned out one of our partners had placed his shoe on my tire to give Galen the advantage. I burned a hole in the shoe and still won the race! It was 2:00 in the afternoon and we were both so exhausted that we could barely walk. Galen made the decision that we should go back to Marriott Hotel and drink… which we did. After our recovery, the scotch helped, Galen proclaimed "House why don't you get some girls." It was more of a challenge than a request. I immediately got up and went out into the lobby, because there were no women in the bar at 3:30 in the afternoon. I did not want to return empty handed! What was I going to do?

Then I noticed a series of phone booths and I detected from a distance that two young women were in the booth together, apparently making a phone call. I got a crazy idea! I began to pick up my pace in the direction of the phone booth and as I got closer I broke into a run. As I reached the booth and moved into the open door, I proclaimed that I was Superman and that there was an emergency, all as I was attempting to unbutton and remove my shirt. It was crazy! Five minutes later I walked into the bar with a beautiful Texas girl on each arm. When Galen noticed me, he got out of his chair, then stood up on the center of our table and began to applaud. I had brought an entire new meaning to the world of Superman!

In the early seventies, woman's fashion shows were pretty traditional. A recognized member of our community in good standing would dress up at our local country club, walk out, do a curtsy and someone would read from a card a description of the dress, handbag and other accessories… it was usually a rather boring event.

I remember when the movie came out called "Close Encounters of a Third Kind." Right there at the end of the movie, I decided to have a fashion show that would be different. The invitation would read "Clothes Encounters of a Fall Kind". I convinced a new friend who owned a lumber yard to economically build, an eight-section stage using 4' x 4' sections of plywood. The design was perfect, especially when they became bolted together with a carpeted surface. I rented the VFW Center which would accommodate an audience of 250 people. I planned to have my daughter, Melanie (Barb and I had divorced, and I was remarried to Jan, who I had known from the University of Iowa. Jan had two children from a prior marriage, which became mine through formal adoption) with her best friend (both gymnasts) begin the show with flips on the stage. Next, we had hired three models from Minneapolis who would come out on stage in a vibrant dance routine and change/exchange clothes in front of the audience, wearing bikinis as under garments. The 200 plus audience responded enthusiastically! I had convinced a local stereo shop owner to put in a fabulous sound system for our event. We had seven different high-end vendors doing trunk shows, highlighted by a Chicago Furrier! Amazingly, we sold twenty seven mink and fox jackets that night. It was an outstanding success.

I was doing pretty well as a ladies ready-to-wear buyer, until on an airplane to New York, I met the owner of a very successful Minnesota women's store chain. He convinced me to consider the installment of a lingerie department. His brother was the president of Form Fit Rogers… at that time the Victoria Secret of New York. My new friend arranged an appointment for me later that week. When I entered one of the most elaborate facilities that I had ever seen, I was immediately and warmly greeted by the Form Fit Rogues president and escorted to a magnificent show room. Almost immediately a parade of beautiful models wearing nothing, but their lingerie began the process of vividly displaying their merchandise. I ended up with a huge order that would take me two years to sell (liquidate) even with serious mark downs.

I learned a good lesson…don't buy with emotion; buy with an analytic foundation.

Another fun story (a learning experience on being impulsive) occurred during an automobile trip to our Marshall Minnesota headquarters for a manager/owner meeting. As I was returning to Fairmont, I noticed a "Horse for Sale" sign on the roadside and I decided to stop by and check it out. My horse at that time was getting older and had suffered a leg injury that winter. I had driven home early to our South Silver Lake compound because of a major blizzard. Jan suggested that we take our horses for a ride in the snow. Unfortunately, I misjudged the solid part of our horse grate over the driveway and Baccarat (we called him Rat) managed to get his front hoof caught in the grate. The horse freaked out and I was thrown off. I immediately got down on the ground and somehow with unknown strength was able to pull his leg out. Rat immediately reared up and got his left back leg caught in the grate. I was now seeing the picture of being forced to shoot him to end his misery. Somehow I mustered up the energy to get my hands around his rear leg and successfully removed it from the grate. Our veterinarian could not visit Rat until the next day. We cleaned and wrapped up his legs and hoped for the best. Fortunately, his injuries were not serious! Blood was everywhere, but Rat was standing and nothing appeared to be broken. However, I spent the next six months taking diathermetric heat treatments for strains in muscles throughout my entire body.

Now back to the "Horse for Sale" sign! I decided to stop at the farm and discovered a beautiful Arabian, named Justy Mar, who was favorably priced. I was wearing a suit at the time, so I trusted the owner's insights on how well Justy was broken in---a big mistake! After an hour or so with Justy, I trusted my equestrian instincts and decided to buy him. The owners delivered him (probably drugged) the following week. Jan, understandably questioned my judgment, but I was thrilled. Then on a Sunday afternoon for my first ride I was bucked off and fortunately not injured other than my pride. Two of my best friends with extensive horse experience volunteered to break him in and both experienced similar outcomes!

With some good luck I found a farmer ten miles from South Silver that was willing to purchase Justy (an 80% discount from my acquisition price) on the condition that I deliver him. Now we quickly learned that Justy refused to enter our horse trailer. After repeated efforts, I convinced a neighbor who had raised Quarter horses to help me load Justy. Our plan was to back the horse trailer up to the large barn door and close every other exit and force Justy into the trailer. After two hours of exhausting exercise we gave up! Therefore, I decided to transport Justy on foot with a halter and a strong lead rope to his new home. Ten miles for a horse was nothing; for me it was a long distance. As we commenced our road trip, down our half mile long drive way, Justy decided that he preferred the barn and broke loose and returned to his stall. I was hoping that he might try the lake and discover that he could not swim! I retrieved him and successfully got to the end of our driveway. Jan was there with our truck and the plan was for me to sit on the tailgate, Jan would drive slow and Justy would obediently follow. Good luck with that wish! As we began our trip down the roadside Justy would rear up whenever a car drove by and head for the ditch with me hanging on for dear life! Fortunately, I was wearing leather gloves and I was able to somehow hang on for dear life. After some forward progress, with eight miles to go we encountered a major storm with torrential rains, lightning and thunder! Justy broke loose from me again and ran full speed down the road for approximately three miles----actually a godsend! I was almost hoping that Justy would encounter a fast semi-truck and end up in horse heaven, but despite some heavy traffic he had survived! When we caught up to him he appeared to be absolutely exhausted! At least now he ceased his antics and actually allowed me to lead him down the road. I am not sure who was more drenched and exhausted; me or the horse? When we arrived at Justy's new home he actually seemed pleased. For me it was a good lesson: "Be less impulsive and take the time to think through decisions with some fundamental due diligence before making a good one!"

Through the years we built our organization to nine men's stores and six ladies stores in four states. Business was really good! Although we were highly leveraged. I was in charge of the Fairmont men's store and responsible for overseeing the merchandising of all the ladies stores. We had acquired a corporate airplane to facilitate efficient travel. I became a pilot after a year of intense training! And since my daughter Jackie was in her mother's custody 400 miles away I would fly Jackie to Fairmont as often as possible. Jackie was a real trooper and even helped me navigate, as I would often use water towers in little towns to know where I was, since I have no sense of direction! Without the sun I would not be able to tell you East from West.

One of my first cross country solo flights was to Marshall, Minnesota. I had confidently found the Marshall airport in my Piper Warrior airplane, located next to a golf course. As I approached the airport for landing I noticed the close proximity of power lines, as I simultaneously checked the tetrahedron for wind direction. As I began my landing approach, it seemed like my ground speed was too fast, and when I tried to touch down I knew that I had excessive speed. Accordingly, I gave the 150 horse powered engine full throttle and decided to come around again. This time I applied two notches of flaps to slow me down. It was not a very long runway. As I approached, again, I was going too fast. So I applied full throttle and released my flaps. Immediately the stall warning device sounded, as I nearly stalled the airplane. It was a serious mistake to release the flaps before attaining proper airspeed. Now I am getting concerned. Should I just go back to Fairmount or should I try again? I decided to go for one more attempt. This time I would employ all three notches of flaps and land this plane! Fortunately, I made the landing. As I disembarked from the airplane, with my shirt soaked from nervous sweat, I was greeted by an older gentleman who was the airport part time manager with the question: "What's your name sonny?" As I proudly proclaimed, John House, he immediately responded: "No, you have a new name and from now on you will be called "Downwind John", because you just landed on the wrong way of the runway." I immediately looked at the wind sock and he was right, I had misread it due to a moderate and fluctuating wind... a mistake I would never make again.

Outside of transporting Jackie, I only had one other experience in a family flight. Jan, I think, reluctantly agreed to let me fly our family, which included son Matt, daughter Melanie and our new arrival, daughter Tiffany to Spencer Iowa to the home of Jan's parents. At the time Jackie was in Iowa with her mother.

We took off on a perfect day, and I used my VOR system to find Spencer perfectly. However, like most small-town airports on a golf course, the airport only had one landing strip. On that particular day there was a twenty knot cross wind. By now I am reasonably seasoned as a pilot and I know exactly what I have to do in a cross wind. The plane is being blown away from the runway, so it is necessary to fly the plane aimed into the wind and time the landing so that at touch down the plane is in the middle of the runway flying at an angle into the crosswind. The only issue is the sliding and screeching of the tires when rubber meets concrete. To me it was a landing in which an instructor would have given me a score of ten, to my family it was pretty scary. Had I not been so heavily focused on controlling the plane, I would have warned everyone about the impact results (noise) at touchdown.

I will share one more flight experience that was pretty scary. Our Mankato owner/manager and I had attended a vendor meeting in Marshall, Minnesota, our headquarters. I had flown from Fairmont to Mankato in a Cherokee Arrow plane with a variable pitch propeller, retractable gear and powered with a two hundred horse power engine to accommodate a ride for my Mankato partner. On our return trip about five miles from Mankato we both began to smell smoke. Soon we could see smoke in the air plane, and when we opened a side vent window, the plane cabin began to fill up with smoke. I made a Mayday call to the Mankato airport and fortunately they had a control towner with a part time aviator who happened to be present during my distress call.

As a pilot I had trained "under the hood" (learned to fly with only instruments) but I was still only licensed for VFR… allowed to fly with a Visual Flight Rule mandate.

At this point we could still see the instrument panel, but the outside atmosphere was completely blocked. Our hope to land was in the hands of the control tower. When he made visual contact with our plane, he began giving vector orders on altitude and direction. The smoke was worse, but we hung in there! As we approached the landing strip, our new friend form the tower had us coming in perfectly on target. As we landed we could hear the siren of a firetruck that was close by on the approach runway. We had safely landed! It turned out that a wiring short had caused insulation in the door to smolder, thereby creating the toxic smoke. We both thanked God for our lives and felt truly blessed on that day!

Another more down to earth fun experience occurred when Aspen Eagle of Ajax, my 75 pound Springer Spaniel, and I were sent to Sherborn, Minnesota to pick up and bring home a four wheeled trailer that contained 120 bales of freshly harvested hay for our horses. I had acquired my used pickup truck from a veterinarian, who owned a pig farm. I had employed two full bottles of Old Spice on the floor of the truck in an effort to eliminate the smell to no avail!! However, I don't think that the odor bothered Aspen very much. He was just happy to be included in the ride! When you pull a fully loaded hay wagon the maximum speed is not much more than ten miles per hour. As a farm oriented community, most people were tolerant of tractors and hay wagons on the highway. The twenty five mile return trip was going to take a long time and I was glad that I had Aspen as my companion! As I approached the town of Sherborn, approximately twenty miles from our home, I decided to stop and buy a six pack of Coors Light---my favorite beer, since visiting the Coors factory in college. Whenever I traveled with Aspen I would bring his water dish and today was no exception. After a beer or two I decided to see if Aspen would drink beer? I stopped and poured out the water and replaced it with a warm beer. Amazingly, he seemed to like it better than his water as it quickly disappeared. As we proceeded down the road with Aspen sitting right next to me (he refused to wear his seat belt), I decided to do a modest wolf howl and as I concluded Aspen piped in with one of his best howls! Therein began a serious contest wherein we were seriously trying to out howl each other. I think in retrospect that Aspen won the contest! It was fun to watch the reaction of all the people that passed us! We even received a nod of appreciation from a Martin County Highway Patrolman as he passed us!

Being in a small town it was both easy and fun to get involved. I spent three years as the chairman of the Board of Fairmont Growth Opportunities and during my term we landed three new industries, including the Toro Lawnmower Company for our 35,000 square foot (empty) speck building. I got the chance to make friends with several dignitaries, including Rudy Boschwitz, who was one of our two Minnesota Senators. His family owned Plywood Minnesota, a smaller version of Home Depot.

I was also the chairman of the Board Directors of our Church for two years. I will never forget the intense meetings, whereupon I was being the analytic and preaching budget while others would proclaim, let's do it anyway (spend the money) and God will take care of it.

As we entered the eighties it became pretty challenging. Interest rates had escalated. Our ten-year lease was approaching maturity. After several months of negotiations with Galen, he allowed me to buy out his interest for a ten year note and a modest down payment. We were strapped for cash! I did have a contingency plan. While acting has the Chairman of Fairmont Growth Opportunity's, I had been successful in negotiating with Burlington Railroad to extend a branch to our Industrial Park. I was persistent. Without the rail access we would have never landed the three new industries that ultimately located in our Industrial Park!

Simultaneous to my railroad negotiations in Chicago, I was making an all-out effort to purchase a defunct Texaco gas station property located at the front of our shopping center. I perceived it as the new location for Wilsons and dimension when our lease ended. After more than a year of negotiations, Texaco Corporation accepted my offer. There was only one problem, where would I get the $120,000 purchase price?

When I went to our banker he made an offer we could not refuse. He would support and honor our purchase agreement, on the condition that I would lease First National Bank the property for thirty years with a competitive lease that would be indexed. For that he would lend me the $120,000 and we could use the lease payment to pay off the loan. I had visions of seeing our four children's educational funding, as a done deal! Of course, I accepted the offer.

Simultaneously, I made the decision to buy an old building in downtown Fairmount as an ultimate exit strategy from the Shopping Center mall. The price was right, and it was a good location. There were three levels and a full basement. The fourth level had rotted away leaving a naked elevator tower that was being supported by four guide wires attached to the roof. In addition, the building had three different types of stucco and the roof leaked. Without any doubt, it was the ugliest building in the whole of Martin County.

I took it upon myself to accomplish a complete renovation. As evidenced by the photos below of the "before" and "after", the building was not going to be capable of accommodating Wilsons and dimension without a major renovation. I thought if I did some of the work myself, money could be saved. One project that resulted in a ten pound weight loss was the drilling of 145 holes, four inches in diameter, to accommodate insulation on the second floor of the building. That project, in the heat of summer (no air-conditioning) took me two weeks. Because

I knew all of the contractors personally, I felt confident in the various construction bids. Unfortunately, a number of unforeseen obstacles were discovered. My mortgage with the local Savings and Loan had to be expanded to accommodate the extra expenditures. The interest rate on my fifteen-year fixed mortgage was 18.0%! Even at that high level monthly payments would be 50% of what the shopping center wanted for a new lease. Plus, I was now the owner of a building for better or worse. I liked the idea of being my own landlord!

I expected a decrease in sales as compared to the shopping center, due to no Sunday openings and being open only one night per week---Monday evening. The economic environment was near catastrophic! Farm prices had fallen drastically. And, foreclosures in Martin County became daily events.

During the final months of the Wilson and dimension saga, we ran a very successful Going Out of Business sale that accomplished the redemption most of the bank debt that I had assumed. The success of my liquidation sale was greatly enhanced by nine different wholesaler friends, who voluntarily came to Fairmont with their sample lines of clothing, which they offered at deep pricing discounts. Moreover, many stayed in Fairmont at their own expense and helped us achieve a successful business liquidation. Many were the same folks who I had worked with at Dayton's; the ones I had treated with respect! I was most likely the only retailer that they knew who continued to buy breakfast and lunches until the end of my business! Another good lesson: "What goes around; comes around"!

Finally, I learned the most important lesson of my life: "I thought that I was too good at what I did to ever fail"! Wrong! My tenacity got in the way of good judgment!

On the day before closing both stores (Wilsons and dimension) the Chamber of Commerce was having their annual gala celebration. As the Chamber president, I held a cocktail party at our home for board members and local dignitaries. As I recall, we entertained (the pre-party) over sixty people. Then to the VFW, where my audience would be over 200. I had Mark Dayton, the head of Minnesota Economic Development department as our keynote speaker. Mark, as of this writing is the governor of Minnesota. My role was to provide an economic update and introduce Mark. Most everyone knew that I had failed in my plight to maintain our retail operation and both stores were actually closing the very next day!

When I walked up to the podium from the head table, I spent fifteen seconds looking at my audience and then I delivered one of my best speeches ever! I was upbeat and confident. My presentation was well received! The next day I left my family for Minneapolis, where I had accepted a commission only job with CIGNA Financial. I was entering the Financial Services industry with one of the best organizations in the country.

With no money, and my wife Jan (at that time) supporting us with her successful operation of the Gingerbread house---(a pre-school located at our church with 40 kids), I lived with my brother.

CIGNA had a minimum planning fee of $5000 in 1982. I did not know any better. I was told to cold call business owners and to achieve eight to ten appointments per week. My goal was simply defined by three life circumstances or results at each meeting:

1. Obtain a document (financial statement or a tax return or a copy of a buy/sell agreement) at the conclusion of my approach talk
2. Get a date to have the next meeting to take Data (financial information)
3. Or get kicked out of the office!

Mostly, I was subjected to Number 3 and asked to leave!

During my first month of work, CIGNA was celebrating their Annual Recognition event for their Agent/Registered Representatives at the prestigious Edina Country Club. As a rookie (a member of the New Organization or New Org) I was invited to attend.

When it came time for our Reginal Vice President to recognize the three of us as New Org members, I was duly impressed with his personal observations on my two counterparts. However, when he came to me, he boldly announced to the entire group that John has three things going against him:

1. He has moved here from a distant community and does not really know anyone in the Minneapolis or St. Paul community
2. He has no background in securities or insurance, as a men's and ladies' ready-to-wear retailer
3. And, as a result of closing his retail operations, faced a challenging financial environment

I was a little surprised by his third statement. I think our leader felt I needed to be reminded of the obstacles that we all faced.

One week later an attorney from CIGNA's Hartford home office came in for a presentation. During his talk he shared a story about a successful Registered Representative in Denver. The individual had convinced a bank to refer customers to him through a fee sharing arrangement. As I am sitting in the audience, essentially naked from a client perspective, I decided right there to find a Minneapolis Bank that would refer business to me. I began the next week calling bank presidents. After numerous rejections, I finally got an appointment with Jim Hearon, the Chairman of National City Bank. The appointment for a lunch meeting was at the Minneapolis Club, one of the most prestigious organizations in Minneapolis. I knew enough to know that membership was both exclusive and very expensive!

The title of this book "Synchronicity" originated from this next chapter in my life. Things do happen for a reason. I was struggling… five horses, two dogs, a cat and four children to support certainly provided motivation. I was essentially approaching the greatest financial challenge of my life in a business totally unrelated to my experience!

CHAPTER FOUR

My major concern in convincing National City Bank to provide me with viable referrals was the expected question form Mr. Hearon during our introductory interview: "Well, John tell me how long have you been doing this?" *My answer of four weeks would certainly close the door before it opened.*

As we met each other in the lobby of the Minneapolis Club, we were escorted to an absolutely beautiful dining area. The dining rooms ambiance was both warm and professional. Just as Mr. Hearon and I were exchanging niceties, I was approached by my only fraternity brother in Minneapolis, Michael Cunningham. Michael at that time was the chairman of Gray Plant Mooty Mooty & Bennett, a prestigious Minnesota Law firm.

Ironically, Jim Hearon's bank was their client and Jim knew Michael personally. Michael provided a warm greeting and then joined another guest for lunch. As I returned to my chair, fear had diminished somewhat, yet I knew that the question on my vocational longevity was soon to be asked.

Then out of nowhere, Rudy Ely Boschwitz walks over to our table. Rudy was our US senator and the founder of Plywood Minnesota. I had met Rudy through my leadership and involvement with Fairmont Growth Opportunities, Inc. (Fairmont Go). He had attended the inauguration and Grand Opening of Toro's lawnmower production facility in our industrial park, an industry that I helped recruit.

Rudy gave me a warm greeting and then began a brief conversation with Mr. Hearon… they seemed to be close friends! Woah! This was too good to be true!

I returned to my chair and began to get comfortable again. Someone had approached me from behind and with his arms around my shoulders was lifting me out of my chair. At first, I thought might be a case of mistaken identity. As it turned out it was my old boss from Dayton's… Ken Macke! Ken was now the Chairman and CEO of Dayton Hudson's Department Stores and Target Corporation! Certainly, Mr.

Big on the Minneapolis Campus. Ken gave me a warm greeting and then I introduced Ken to Mr. Hearon. They exchanged some meaningful comments and Ken proceeded to his meeting. Woah again!

Ironically, the bank Chairman never asked me the longevity question and essentially agreed to consider a referral program with a fee sharing arrangement. The formal release letter appears below.

NATIONAL CITY BANK
OF MINNEAPOLIS

P.O. Box 81919 • Minneapolis, Minnesota 55480
Telephone (612) 340-3000

We have referred you to CIGNA Securities in connection with their personal financial planning services. The purpose of this letter is to make sure that you are aware of our relationship with CIGNA Securities and its affiliates.

With respect to the personal financial planning services of CIGNA Securities, we act solely in a referral capacity. CIGNA Securities, as a registered financial advisor, is solely responsible for their financial planning services. In the event that you enter into a personal financial planning contract with CIGNA Securities, CIGNA Securities will pay us a referral fee out of the Personal financial Planning Contract fee agreed to by CIGNA Securities and you. The referral fee is identified on the fee schedule attached to the planning contract and is one component of the advisory fee charged by CIGNA Securities. The advisory fee of CIGNA may vary based on a number of factors including income and net worth of the client.

Please sign the enclosed copy of this letter and return it to CIGNA Securities in the envelope provided thereby acknowledging receipt of this letter as well as receipt of their Disclosure Brochure.

Sincerely,

Receipt Acknowledged:

____
(Client Signature) (Date)

John A. House
Registered Representative

CIGNA Securities, Inc.
Registered Investment Advisor
6800 France Avenue South, Suite 600
Minneapolis, Minnesota 55435

It took only three months for our CIGNA attorneys to negotiate the terms and conditions of our joint venture with National City's Bank's attorneys. The Bank's attorneys came up with a "Disclosure Agreement" that would satisfy the regulatory community. On every fee arrangement that CIGNA wrote, as a Registered Investment Advisory (RIA) organization the Bank could receive 25% and CIGNA would retain 75%. The bank agreed to identify 126 of their business owner clients, with a net worth in excess of $1,000,000 and a salary of $150,000 or more, AND they would set the appointment for me.... a true marketing panacea!!

I immediately recognized one significant deficiency----my lack of technical expertise and planning knowledge. CIGNA had great training and outstanding support, but I decided to do my best to become technically competent in the fields of finance and tax law. We were always careful to communicate to clients that we were not allowed under SEC rules to provide tax or legal advice. However, the more I could learn in each of those fields the better I would be as a financial advisor to high net worth business owners—my target market. Consequently, I spent the next six months, every night in an in-depth study. I would frequently arrive at my brother's residence after midnight and be at the office by 5:00 am the next morning. I think that I read "Tax Facts" (an industry training manual) three times. To this day I try my best to keep current on tax legislation and estate planning techniques. My calendar is constantly filled with various educational conferences around the country! I am known by our Broker/Dealer to be an extremely "technically competent" financial advisor. Therein, is the name of our firm.....MasterTech Financial Advisors. I make a strong effort to "master" the "technical" elements of our industry, always focusing on my ability to properly advise our clients.

As a result of the CIGNA/National City Bank referral program, my production of revenue ranked me number two in the country in my second year of doing business. During my first year, which was also financially productive, I was invited to a special one-week training program in New York that was sponsored by CIGNA and featured our top producers from around the country. It was an amazing event that dramatically enhanced my efforts to become technically competent. I returned with a higher level of confidence ready to embrace the business owner marketplace.

Ironically, the next year I was invited again to the New York event, this time as a featured speaker. When I arrived at LaGuardia, I discovered a man with a poster that contained my name. He was the limo driver that would provide the two-hour ride to Up-State New York, where the program was being held. I had been allotted two hours for my presentation. Nervous does not begin to describe my emotional perspective. Here I was in an environment with CIGNA's seasoned professionals and I was considered sufficiently proficient to address a crowd of eighty individuals who had been awarded attendance, wow! I remember well the ending of my presentation, which focused on client closing techniques. Our process was so well founded, that actually "selling" an investment or insurance product never really occurred. We would spend considerable time asking good questions and then employ empathetic listening to capture the true goals and objectives of our clients. Next, we would focus on understanding planning and life values, as the foundation of the subjective elements. Our training then moved us toward obtaining an accurate picture of the present situation....the current plan or lack thereof. We would review all relevant business and tax related information, as well as complete testamentary documents. We were taught to identify planning deficiencies and risk factors. I often called them "Obstacles and Problems" and when I felt rather kind I would use the term "Planning Opportunities". The idea was to disturb our client with the present situation if circumstances warranted the same. Finally, through a team approach we would develop strategic recommendations that included both planning techniques and necessary insurance and investment products. Consequently, the sale, if you wish, was accomplished by the actual implementation of the Plan. Candidly, thirty-three years later the "process" has not changed. Successful individuals want someone who they can trust, who is reasonably competent and who really cares about them.

My conclusion of the New York presentation exemplified the above referenced principles and our implementation procedure----or the actual close. I decided to employ an example from my days as a menswear retailer. When I presented a high end suit to a male customer, I knew who the decision maker was. The man may do most of the talking, but his wife controls (often subtly) everything. Nothing is different in the financial services industry. Since the vast majority of my clients who own businesses are married, I focus much of my communication and educational efforts on the wife. I want her to pose good questions and get involved in the planning process. Often, I find myself asking the husband, politely, if it is okay for his wife to offer her perspective? Now, back to my closing comments, at the conclusion of the New York presentation. I moved away from the podium and asked my audience to pretend that were inside a men's store, and I was the owner of the establishment. Seasoned retailors understand that the most important element of a man's suit is the fit. Certainly, alterations can enhance, but it is essential that the garment structure is appropriate for the man's physic.

I held in my left hand a piece of tailoring chalk and asked the audience to participate in my close as I positioned the man in front of the mirror after convincing him to try on the pants, an absolute prerequisite. His wife is standing behind him as I kneel down on one knee and look up to her and ask the key question: "Ma'am, would you like this to have a plain bottom or cuff?" She would usually contemplate for a moment and offer her opinion and I would immediately chalk the leg and let the man know that he can get back into his street clothes. The suit was sold! Similar to obtaining client authorization from a detailed implementation schedule, the planning strategies and products recommended in our master game plan would be accepted as key components of the process.

In addition, to the Banks introduction of business owner prospects, I constantly looked for ways to expand our business model through innovative marketing endeavors. Early in my financial service career, I attended an Asset Protection workshop held at the Hilton Hotel in Minneapolis. I was surprised by the size of the audience…over 200 individuals were in attendance. The speaker, Jay Mitton, was an attorney with an MBA in finance. He shared from the podium his life story, which focused on frequent creditor issues for his parents and financial deprivation. His mission was to sell books and CD's on Asset Protection techniques with the ultimate goal of acquiring new clients for his Provo, Utah Law Firm. Surprisingly, I witnessed more than fifty five seminar participants pay $2500 for his asset protection program.

After his presentation I walked up to Jay and made an effort to introduce myself, and he walked away to my surprise! Since "pleasant persistence" and "tenacity" are two of my stronger traits, I decided to attend the same program the very next day in St. Paul. This time I was better prepared.

At the conclusion of the event, I found Jay and put two checks in front of him. One was a new investment account for $5,000,000 (name whited out) and the other was a $250,000 check for a life insurance premium (name whited out). I got Jay's attention and we began a productive dialogue. Making a long story short, I was invited to Provo Utah to meet with the principals of his Law firm. After an in-depth interview, we negotiated an agreement whereupon I could purchase the names of the individuals who acquired the Asset Protection material, around the country, for $100 per name. Writing the first check for $5500 was a little scary. Although, when Ole's wife, her daughter and son-in-law (my first Jay Mitton prospect) came in for an introductory interview, I gained confidence. It turned out that two months prior to our meeting, Ole, who owned a large St. Paul domiciled Tank Company, was shoveling his driveway after a February snow fall at age 88 and died immediately from a massive cardiac arrest. To accomplish the successful transfer of this fifty million-dollar business from Ole's wife (at her demise) to his two daughters and two sons, important Estate Planning was required. We used an approved element of the tax code to establish fractional discounts on the Tank Company stock price, due to lack of marketability and control, and then initiated a gifting program. Ole's spouse was in reasonably good health and we acquired in an Irrevocable Trust a $10,000,000 life insurance policy to help pay the confiscatory estate tax that would be due at her death. It turned out to be a very productive case! We helped install Buy/Sell agreements for the three children who were active in the business and developed a technique to make financially whole the daughter who was not active in the business.

Jay Mitton spoke all over the United States and I knew that I was only one person, so I recruited other CIGNA Registered Representatives to help me. Travel was exhausting, but the new clients were dynamic and in need of competent planning counsel. I chose to limit my exposure to the states that I liked.

One of my favorite clients, a Lasik Surgeon, who attended a special medical conference in Seattle was attracted to Jay's program by a male model who was wearing a Suit of Armor and carrying a sign titled "Asset Protection Planning". I remember well my introductory interview with this doctor and his wife at a downtown Seattle hotel. His story is featured in one of the first chapters of my book "Spellbound by Financial Reality."

Our next major promotional effort was dedicated to the production of video that would feature a local estate planning attorney, a dynamic CPA and four of my clients in a ten-minute interview. Previously, I had produced from a vendor a marketing packet (called an audio business card) that contained a five-minute cassette tape presentation and featured my picture on the front cover. That was easy compared to having CIGNA's compliance team oversee a film production. The $45,000 expenditure turned out to be a good one as a result of how well prospective clients and other advisors responded to our client oriented marketing campaign. The title "Here Today, Gone Tomorrow" featured a family who had experienced the premature death of the husband (age 46) who was the president of a successful plastic manufacturing company. His story is also represented by a chapter in "Spellbound by Financial Reality"!

In the mid-nineties, I was recruited by a head hunter representing Swenson Anderson Financial Group, a prestigious local financial service firm, who was looking for a seasoned estate planner, who could compliment their existing organization. When I met with Dan Anderson, and Wayne Swenson, I was immediately impressed by their enthusiasm and desire to grow their firm. Both men were sons of ministers and reflected solid Christian values. Dan, at nearly seven feet in height was a former NBA player. Their market reputation was flawless and as I later learned, their personal integrity qualities permeated the firm. An ethical approach and focus on the client's best financial interests dominated their every endeavor.

I decided to accept their offer and began my preparations for a transition. My motivation was twofold in perspective. I really felt good about the opportunity working with a local independent firm vs a large national company. Plus, earlier that year I had been asked by Larry English, CIGNA Financials president to join five other Registered Representatives and six Regional Vice Presidents to serve on a Leveraged Buy Out (LBO) committee to find a buyer for the financial services division of CIGNA. The business experience and group comradery was enjoyable, as we met with prospective buyers and learned about complex, leveraged transactions. For me it was another whole world! I can remember a meeting in Chicago with Fireman's Fund's Chairman, where our LBO Leader (a New York Merger Acquisition guru, who we had hired) was late for our meeting.

When he arrived, he immediately complained that his wife had taken their Leer Jet to a golf tournament in North Carolina and he had to fly commercial to Chicago. Now that's a good excuse for being late to a meeting! I remember well our last LBO Committee meeting in recognition of our work (even though we had failed to recruit a qualified buyer) in New York. Larry English took over the top floor of a hotel to celebrate our combined efforts together for a truly amazing experience!

Given the expected ownership volatility for CIGNA was the second reason that I chose to join the stable Swenson Anderson Financial Group. Getting there was not easy. CIGNA as a fiduciary maintained detailed copies of each client's fee-based plan. Plus, there was some ambiguity as to who actually owned the client's files. Accordingly, I spent several weeks between 2:00 AM and 5:00 AM carefully removing my file copies to my Minnetonka residence. When I formally resigned from CIGNA, my three-car garage was jammed with tables that represented the complete records for each of my clients.

I promoted my transition to Swenson Anderson Financial with an announcement that I was not "horsing around" in my business decision to move my financial consulting practice. See below the photo in front of my new office building in downtown Minneapolis.

As it turned out Dan Deegan, CIGNA's Regional Vice President graciously accepted my resignation and the issue of who owned the files never was discussed.

Two years later CIGNA sold their business to Lincoln Financial, causing me to feel really good about my exit decision!

CHAPTER FIVE

During my last year with CIGNA, I encountered an interesting case that could have changed the dynamics of my personal financial life. An Edina, Minnesota client and good friend had asked me to fly to Hong Kong for an introduction to a Moore Stephens accountant (an English accounting firm) who represented a curb and gutter construction company in mainland China. Fortunately, I had a good working relationship with Barbra Hauser, a Minneapolis attorney who spoke fluent Chinese. She became an integral part of our team as we worked with a Scotland domiciled Insurance Company to acquire a large annuity contract that would represent one component of the agreement between the contractor and the Chinese Government. The "deal" was predicated upon combining tax deferral with a guaranteed twenty-year payment of $12,000,000 per year. To accomplish the same, the insurance company required a deposit of $150,000,000 to fund the Immediate Annuity.

I had convinced Barbara to work with me on a contingency basis, whereupon I would share 10% of the expected annuity commission with her. At that time, the proposed commission was 3.0% on a twenty-year period certain annuity contract. As we approached the closing at 3:00 AM Minneapolis time on a Wednesday morning in June of 1991, I had made careful arrangements with my bank to accept the $4,500,000 wire transfer. You can imagine our excitement after six months of frequent and intense negotiations as we approached the closing. As we began the final stages of the transaction, we learned that in Scotland, based upon government statues, the tax deferral component is only ten years on an immediate annuity, contrary to US insurance statue that permits a twenty year period of deferral. The accounting firm in England concluded that without the extra ten years of tax deferral, even though the payment was guaranteed for twenty years, the proposal was unacceptable! The tax consequence to their client would be burdensome and the deal fell-through!

We here in America, were totally crushed… the anticipated wire transfer would never occur! All our work was for naught!

It was a good lesson in financial humility…one that I would never forget.

CHAPTER SIX

Now as I commenced my new role with Swenson Anderson Financial Group and a new Broker/Dealer, we had to obtain approval from each investment client to authorize the transfer of assets. Fortunately, my good relationships with my client base prevailed and eventually 100% of our files were re-registered with Financial Network Investment Corporation (FNIC).

I later learned that I was the first Registered Representative with Swenson Anderson not to be required to participate in a three-month mandatory orientation program, plus I was awarded large office space right next to Dan and Wayne's offices. My relocation caused a senior Swenson Anderson producer with a PHD to move. We ironically met for the first time on a Sunday afternoon, as he was in the final stage of transferring his files to a different office, and immediately become friends. Typical of

Swenson Anderson Associates, benevolence prevailed. Instead of resenting my intrusion, he welcomed me!

My years at Swenson Anderson were truly blessed. Based upon a number of family events, I began to develop some clients in Scottsdale, using Jay Mitton's Asset Protection Leads as the foundation of my initial marketing efforts. I eventually rented an office from my good friend, Bill Jansick, who was now an American Family Agent in Scottsdale. Bill and I had met back when I operated Wilsons and dimension in Minnesota. I acquired some great office furniture and hung my shingle. The first year we decided to rent an apartment and then eventually acquired our Pinnacle Peak residence.

One of the fundamental components of our move to Arizona, was when two gentlemen knocked at the door of our Minnetonka horse property and asked if we were interested in selling. I said no, not at this time and one of the developers responded with an outrageous figure as a proposed starting point and I immediately said come on in! The Minnetonka property became six lots for a high end residential development, which allowed Jan and I to acquire an adobe-built home on five acres in North East Scottsdale, a place today referred to as the compound.

During my first year in Scottsdale I interviewed several estate planning attorneys in an effort to establish a referral relationship. Fortunately, I was introduced to Tax Attorney Tom Dietrich and we immediately began to work together.

In 2005 I decided to build a guest house on our five acre property that would be utilized as an office. It turned out to be a profitable adventure, until 2014 when I joined Tom Dietrich in commercial office space. My daughter Tiffany, who had worked for me on a part time basis began her college endeavors at the University of Arizona in Tucson. One of my client's sons whose family is featured in a chapter in "Spellbound by Financial Reality" introduced me to his New Zealand Fly fishing partner, who now owned a resort in Montana. Conrad's great grandfather had been one of the founders of General Electric and he was interested in doing some planning with GE Stock that he had inherited. On his first two-day trip to Arizona, I introduced him to my daughter, Tiffany, because I thought that we needed a break from each other. Tiffany was home from college.

The next thing you know, Tiffany is married to Conrad and he became my business partner. Now divorced, with three wonderful daughters, Conrad is operating a different business, but we remain good friends. Tiffany began working for our firm and ultimately replaced Conrad as my partner. A lot of our work involves philanthropic planning strategies.

Interestingly, I was introduced to a planning group in Grand Rapids Michigan that had developed a unique charitable planning strategy. One of the principals of the Grand Rapids firm became a good friend. I was asked to be a featured speaker at several meetings and we began dialogue on strategic planning that could help charitable organizations. As it turned out my partner to be was working with a Wells Fargo Vice President, who was interested in expanding a business owner program that focused on a high-tech approach offering employees merchandise and service discounts. Ultimately, after lengthy legal negotiations, we formed a joint venture with Wells Fargo. We had convinced the bank that this Affinity Program would be more productive for donors of charitable organizations, due to their passion for a cause, whereas employees of a large business enterprise (the bank's target market) were less motivated.

We believed that with the use of Wells Fargo's name, we could present this program to large nationally based charities like the Salvation Army and the March of Dimes.

I had previously helped the March of Dimes, as one of their philanthropic advisors, to promote Charitable Remainder Trusts.

Ironically, four weeks into the relationship a Wells Fargo senior manager decided to terminate the program. We were baffled, but we still firmly believed that we could make a real difference for the charitable community. We decided as partners to form an S-Corporation and start our own business. We convinced Tiffany to join us as our salaried executive director. Next, we traveled to New York to renegotiate contracts with the six different affinity vendors. We essentially replicated the terms and conditions that Wells Fargo had achieved on the premise that we were taking the program national. We enjoyed a viable friendship with a gentleman who operated a private foundation enterprise for accomplished (name brand) professional athletes. We also recruited a South Dakota professional Fundraising/Advisory firm as a partner. It took several weeks of negotiations to arrive at a legal relationship sufficient to protect everyone's interests, as well as provide a fair compensatory arrangement.

We then recruited a vendor with a company that set airline employee hotel reservations around the world. Our biggest challenge and expense was the software development to make everything seamless and functional on cell phones. Our final vendor provided emergency worldwide jet service for accident or medical circumstances. The offering contained a large variety of services that would each generate revenue for the charitable organization who sponsored our Affinity Program. We knew that it worked because our central New York vendor had his program working for UPS, Citi Bank and a large manufacturing company. After several months of recruitment, we were finally able to convince the Las Vegas chapter of the Salvation Army to put our Pharmacy Card, designed to discount drug purchases for nine of their stores. I met with the Salvation Army director of the Western Region in Los Angeles to share the results of our pilot program, which were very positive. We also had received favorable results with a Michigan Teachers Association.

Unfortunately, despite an all-out marketing effort, we were unable to successfully launch the program. We remain as an organization capable of helping charities educate their board members and donors on advanced charitable planning strategies. Many good relationship lessons were learned as we generated a major financial effort to succeed.

Subsequent to my separation/divorce in 2014, I have opened an office in Carlsbad, California and continue to work with clients around the country. Tom Dietrich accepted a merger and acquisition position as we simultaneously convinced a prestigious Phoenix Law Firm, Frazer Ryan and Goldberg to share in our Scottsdale office space.

As evidenced by the photo below, I am actively promoting my business and this book.

CONCLUDING OBSERVATIONS

As I continue to grow my business and successfully represent existing and new clients, we focus our emphasis on educational endeavors designed to help protect the financial integrity of our client's assets, as well as mitigate or resolve identified risks and contingencies. With a strong focus on successful tax planning, we are often able to eliminate estate taxes and dramatically reduce income taxes!

If you have not yet watched my Nasdaq video, representative of a unique client experience, I encourage you to do so. The tax results accomplished by this client, combined with his contribution to society are dynamic!

SOME PERSONAL THOUGHTS ON EMOTIONAL WELL-BEING IN LIFE

Our many past accomplishments, loving memories, self-afflicted pain, mistakes, and choices are forever gone. Because the past is gone, we know it is best not to dwell on our prior history; rather learn from it.

It is never easy for us to judge our behavior and conduct from the perspective or in the eyes of others, who we really care about. We cannot control their perceptions of us! As we know, true happiness comes from within; not from other's opinions, actions, beliefs, or behaviors.

Our thoughts, ultimately become "things". Because we can control our thoughts, we are smart to manifest desired outcomes and practice optimism.

Since all we really have is the present moment, dwelling on the past can be dysfunctional and frustrating.

The secret of emotional well-being is to discount the good opinion of others and live your life unencumbered.

You cannot possibly love another on this earth completely, until you love yourself unconditionally.

SOME FAMOUS QUOTES THAT I LIKE

"The more I understand myself, the more effectively I can work with others."

-Zig Ziglar

"Forgiveness is the scent that the rose leaves on the heel that crushes it."

-Dr. Wayne Dyer

"There is only one way to avoid criticism: do nothing, say nothing, and be nothing."

-Aristotle

"Believe you can and you're halfway there."

-Theodore Roosevelt

"In order to succeed, your desire for success should be greater than your fear of failure."

Albert Schweitzer

"I've learned that people will forget what you said, people will forget what you did, but people will not forget how you made them feel."

-Maya Angelou

"If you cannot do great things, do small things in a great way!"

-Napoleon Hill

"You must keep your mind on the objective, not the obstacle."

-William Randolph Hearst

"Only those who do nothing never make a mistake."

-Mikhail Gorbachev

"Life isn't about finding yourself. Life is about creating yourself."

-George Bernard Shaw

"Every strike brings me closer to the next home run."

-Babe Ruth

"Life is 10% what happens to me and 90% of how I react to it."

-Charles Swindoll

"Winning isn't everything, but wanting to win is."

-Vince Lombardi

"What once appeared to us as difficulties and challenges, now often reveal themselves as real blessings."

-John House

"I am not a product of my circumstances; I am a product of my decisions."

-Stephen Covey

"He is no fool who gives up what he cannot keep in order to gain what he cannot lose."

-Author Unknown

"Communication is a receiver based phenomena."

-<u>Madalyn Engle</u>

"The problem with communication is the illusion that is has occurred."

-<u>George Bernard Shaw</u>

"Authentic leadership only occurs when one both discovers and then manifests the true potential from others."

-<u>John House</u>

HOUSEISMS

- Expand your horizons by always maintaining an optimistic outlook.
- You *choose* your reaction to every life event based upon your perception, which tends to be your reality!
- You create your own destiny.
- Honesty *prevails* over everyone and everything.
- Learn from the past, but focus on the present.
- Never forget what is *worth* remembering, but do forget to remember those experiences in life that are best forgotten.
- Look upon "problems" as *opportunities* which are designed to make you stronger and smarter.
- Remember, no one can change or get better unless they admit that something is wrong.
- People with overly strong opinions are often fearful of their own inadequateness.

- Never give up; tenacity and persistence prevail over any other form of human behavior.
- Avoid being against anything; instead be for something.
- Without the realization and development of your personal faith, life will become a disappointing experience.
- You're only as good as you think you can be.
- Before you can love anyone else you must first love yourself.
- The most important lifetime effort is dedicated to building long lasting relationships.
- All things are complex, when they are poorly understood.
- Look for and appreciate the faults that cause your friends to be individuals.
- "Laugh at yourself" first, last and often!
- Happiness results from inner freedom, unrestricted trust and giving back to others.
- Successful individuals are unreasonable in the expectations they create for themselves.
- The only real things in life that you can keep are the things you give away.
- What matters is what you do with what you have.
- Through unfettered desire we create the ability to convert dreams to reality.

- Imagination is only limited by experience!
- A pure, untainted *vision* will cause a possibility to become a reality.
- Always remember that the pain of self-discipline is temporary, and the pride of accomplishment is *forever.*
- Hard work and dedication to your principles will make you very lucky.
- The only thing wrong with doing nothing *is* that you never know when you are finished.
- Lost time is never found again; therefore, time is not lost and found.
- Never complain, never explain and never blame, accept responsibility for your own actions.
- If it's worth doing it's worth overdoing.
- Good anticipation (expected outcomes) is the result of strategic preparation. And good preparation overcomes "predefined" boundaries that we often impose upon ourselves.
- Always focus on the "long term" versus "immediate gratification" and realize that success takes time.
- Victory results from conquering our fears.

- Perform more than you have promised, give more than expected and get more than needed.
- Achievers are separated from non-achievers through adoption of disciplined self-management techniques.
- Well-chosen words packed with emotion create incredible results.
- You can't talk yourself out of problems that you behave yourself into.
- Outlook is a function of aspiration.... The only *real limits* we impose are the ones *we believe* to be true.
- Doing something is better than doing nothing.
- Use your "emotions" to think with.
- Ethics is to have the courage to do what is right, even when it represents personal costs.
- Only when the questions become more important than the answers will the solutions emerge.

Printed in the United States
By Bookmasters